Goes for a Ride

HOUGHTON MIFFLIN BOSTON

Printed in India

ISBN-13: 978-0-547-01865-2
ISBN-10: 0-547-01865-7

2 3 4 5 6 7 8 9 0940 15 14 13 12 11 10

George likes to ride on a bike.

He likes to ride
on a sled.

He likes to ride
on a bus.

He likes to ride
in a balloon.

He likes to ride
in a rocket!

Responding

TARGET SKILL Story Structure

Who is the main character in the story? Where does the story happen? What happens? Make a chart.

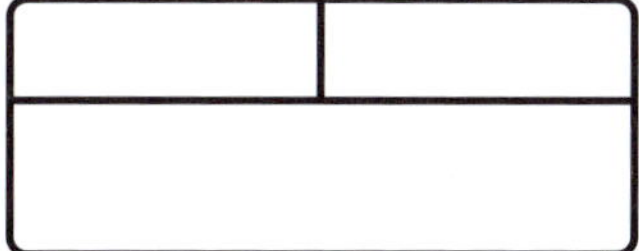

Talk About It

Text to Self Which vehicles in the story have you used? Which one would you like to try? Draw a picture of yourself in that vehicle. Then tell about your picture.

look	out

TARGET SKILL **Story Structure** Tell the setting, characters, and events in a story.

TARGET STRATEGY **Infer/Predict** Use clues to figure out more about story parts.

GENRE **Fiction** is a story that is made up.